MW00960106

The Truth About Santa Claus

Text by Mabel Hauser (1916-1977) ©2018 by Hillary Hauser
Art by Avalo Petri (1910-1980) ©2018 by Hillary Hauser

PUBLISHED BY HILLARYHAUSER.COM BOOKS
HILLARYHAUSER.COM BOOKS
1187 Coast Village Road #288
Santa Barbara, CA 93108

Book Design and Color Illustration Reproduction by Bellman Design, Santa Barbara

©2018 All rights reserved. No part of this publication may be reproduced
in any form or by any means, electronic, mechanical, photocopying, recording
or otherwise, without the prior permission of the publisher.

The Truth About Santa Claus

Text Revived by Hillary Hauser
Color Reproduction by Debbie Bellman

Original Text by Mabel Hauser
Original Art by Avalo Petri

Published by HillaryHauser.com Books
Santa Barbara, California

Dedicated to Young Hearts Everywhere

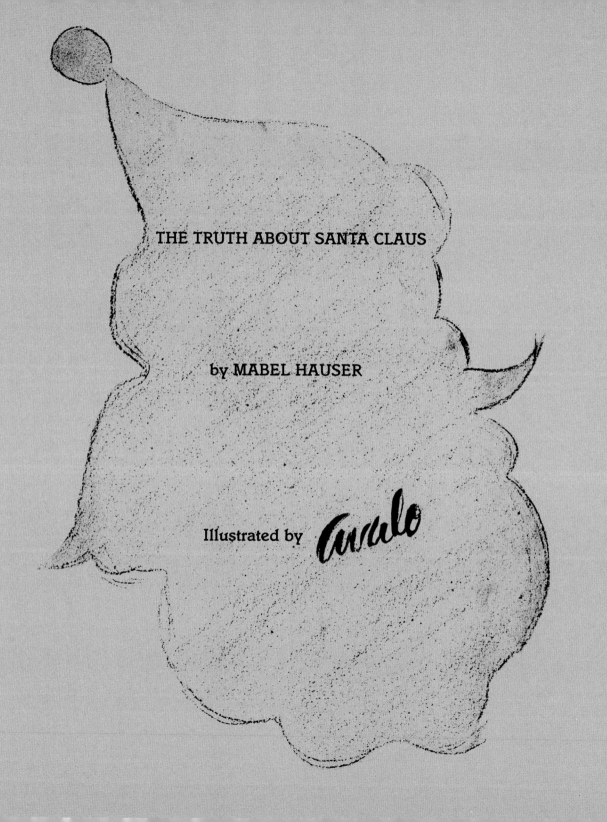

THE TRUTH ABOUT SANTA CLAUS

by MABEL HAUSER

Illustrated by *Avalo*

e do not really see a star,
We see the light that it sends.
The beauty of music can be seen,
Like the wind, by the tree that it bends.
We "see" gladness, joy, peace, and love –
"To see" means to comprehend.

Visions are pictures
Of things that are real
Things seen in symbols
Are things that we feel.

To outline Love's spirit
Would be so hard to do,
But we'll show you the symbols,
and paint them for you!

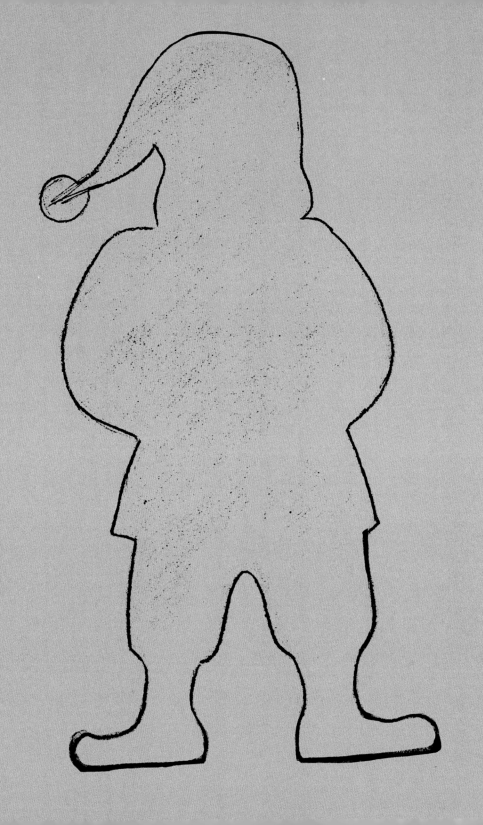

Santa not real?
Why he's ideal!
Didn't folks say
Of the kindly old elf
"He's like
The Spirit of Giving
Itself?"

The Spirit of Giving
Is very old.
(How long, since the Wise Men
Brought Myrrh and Gold!)

Old and Time....
Age and Grace....
White flowing hair
And a beard on his face.

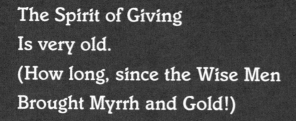

The Spirit of Giving
Is clothed with light
Seen as a color,
It is red and bright!

Abounding in richness
Well stocked with mirth –
A tummy of gladness,
A big belt for girth.

Such overabundance
Is not hard to see –
It's sometimes called fatness
Santa's fat as can be!

Smiling and jolly
Laughing and gay –
When we think of joy,
We "see" it that way.

The Spirit warms
My heart and yours
On Santa Claus
Let's put some furs!

And then his boots...
He has climbing to do
(Joy lifts us as high
As the rooftops, too.)

What else does he need?
A great big pack –
The gifts of Love
We put on his back!

A blanket of snow?
A world pure and white
The Christ idea born
On a star-studded night!

So Santa Claus comes
At the time of the year
When snow seems a part
Of the Christmas cheer.

Faster than lightning
Our thoughts can go –
(A sled is the fastest thing
for snow.)

To pull a sled,
What represents speed?
The perfect thing
That we would need –

Is a soaring team
That flies Santa here –
A string of eight
Beautiful, prancing deer!

With Bells!
Of course!
The peals of joy
When Christ was born
A little boy!

How does he travel?
Fast, through the air!
You and I know
Love flies everywhere.

And night is the time
For this earth-circling flight,
Ideas glimpsed but dimly
Are like beams of starlight.

When the world was in darkness
We didn't know he was there –
But the morning light proves
Santa's been everywhere!

Down the chimney?
Why, don't you know
There isn't a place
Where Love can't go?

For the spirit of giving
Is Love made seen,
And to hearts (and houses)
Great or mean –

Love finds an opening.
In my house and yours,
A chimney for Santa
When we lock up the doors!

You have no chimney...?
Well don't you mind
Love needs no special door
To find.

And Santa Claus
Can come and go
Locked up doors,
Chimney or no.

The men in the stores?
The men on the street?
Alive "pictures" of Santa
That you can meet!
Tell them your wishes,
Have your say
Santa hears as well as they.

Oh Santa is so very Real!
The Spirit of Christmas
That all of us feel!
To describe this Spirit
Would give us pause
So we just say . . . .

It's SANTA CLAUS!

Mabel Hauser (1916-1977) was a housewife and dedicated mother who wrote stories to read to her three children: Merrily, Hillary and Craig Hauser, to present old tales (like opera plots – Lohengrin, Tannhauser) in new ways to encourage childhood wonderment. Her sister, **Avalo Petri** (1910-1980) joined her in making these books, to read to her own children, Pamela ("Pammy") & Stephanie ("Taffy") Petri. The two sisters made the books themselves, in a style of binding where they could read from one side while the corresponding pictures were on the other, facing their children.

Avalo Petri was a noted illustrator, a graduate of the Cornish School of Art in Seattle, Washington. She was chief fashion artist for the Los Angeles Examiner, while producing the Laraine Day and "My Little Margie" coloring books, as well as the Joanne Woodward paper doll books commissioned by the Saalfield Publishing Co. of Akron, Ohio.

Hillary Hauser, a widely published writer in her own right, resurrected a faint, black & white xeroxed copy of "The Truth About Santa Claus" from boxes of old family archival materials, and went to work on the idea of recreating the book made by her mother and aunt. To do this, she enlisted the help of long-time graphic designer **Debbie Bellman**, of **Bellman Design, Santa Barbara**, to reproduce this classic work in a way that adheres as closely as possible to the text, illustrations and intent of the original book, created 70 years ago. The aim of these two enterprising women, Mabel Hauser and Avalo Petri, was to present Santa Claus in a way that Santa can always be enjoyed and celebrated.

Mabel Hauser, reading to her children, 1949

Made in the USA
Coppell, TX
06 December 2021

67297396R00031